New Year New Career: 2014
Part-time gigs or full-time jobs

By Jenny Holmes

New Year New Career: 2014
Copyright © 2013 by Jenny Holmes
Published by: Two Buck eBooks

All rights reserved. No part of this book may be reproduced, stored in a retrieval system or transmitted by any means, electronic, mechanical, photocopying, recording or otherwise without written permission from the author.

Note from the author:
Life is too short to do the same thing every day and 2014 is your best year ever. Crank up your career and do something new and exciting—and get paid to do it. This book offers ideas for cool gigs, unique jobs, new social ways to work from home and jobs that pay you to travel. Whether you are interested in part-time gigs or full-time jobs, this book offers advice and resources on how to get them or CREATE them. Become a consultant, get conference-speaking gigs, be a virtual personal trainer or a professional sleeper for a hotel. Your dream job is out there. This book is a compilation of things I've tried, jobs I've had, freelance gigs, life experiences and some crazy new things on my bucket list. I hope you find your dream gig, your new career or discover a hobby that pays.

I would love to hear your new gig stories. Email me:
Jenny@ThePubPlace.com

Table of Contents

Become a Consultant
Professional Organizer
Immersion Writer
Conference Speaker
Blog
Write a Weekly Column for a Newspaper
Design Websites
Publish a Book
Freelance Social Media
Contract Fundraiser
Fashion Consultant
Online Educator
Tech Consultant
Make and Sell Jewelry
Professional Food Taster or Taste-Tester
Promotional Person
Grant Writer
Review Writer
Teach Abroad
Put Yourself on Tour
Become a Ghostwriter
Bike Tour Guide
Nonprofit Leader
Social Analytics Consultant
Virtual Assistant
Home Call Center
Electronic Clipping Service
Digital Organizer
Photography Organizer
Personal Shopper

- Scarf Maker
- Gift Shop GIFTY Creator
- Recruiter/Hiring Firm
- Wine Glass Painter
- Become a Sommelier
- Crime Scene Cleaner
- Brewmaster
- Professional Sleeper
- Resort Jobs
- Private Investigator
- Body Parts Model
- Phone Actress
- Write for Dumb People
- Fancy Dress Rental
- Toy Tester
- Traveling Artist
- Virtual Fitness Instructor
- Market Researcher
- Zamboni Driver
- Trade Show Organizer
- Gaming Surveillance Observer
- Video Maker for You Tube
- Fluffer

Become a Consultant
You are good at something. I know you are REALLY good at something. Do you love to organize people? Maybe you are a great proofreader or writer? Did you once have a great career in technology? Are you a special event planner or incredible hostess? Maybe you know marketing, web design or grant writing. Or do all your co-workers call you to help with Excel or Microsoft publisher? Sit down right now and write down all the things at which you excel. Then write down those things you are good at and absolutely love. Then go out and sell yourself to organizations that could potentially use your service. To find out about the top thriving consulting businesses, read a recent article in <u>Entrepreneur</u> magazine "How to Start a Consulting Business."

Professional Organizer
People buy crap all year long then wake up and realize they could be on the next episode of hoarders. January is national 'Get organized month,' so it is the perfect time to make some money off other people's messes. You can charge by the room or charge by the house with an average income of $300 to $5,000 per client depending on how messy they are . . . or how much stuff they buy. Nearly a decade ago, I took an online professional organizing course and got the certificate. For $300 I learned how to throw 3 big boxes in every room and label them, "throw it away" "give it away" and "sell it on ebay." So I just saved you several hundred dollars in an organizational how-to class, because you don't need the certificate, just some committed organizational skills and some boxes. Lots of boxes. So post your gig on facebook to get in on the January frenzy. Be creative. Visit Pinterest for clever organizing ideas for every room of the house. Remember to add special touches like color-coding, labels and such. Take before and after photos, so other messy people can see your mad skills and will hire you.

Immersion Writer
Somewhere in your town there is a local newspaper or 'area' newspaper looking for freelance writers. Offer to have experiences, then write about them. The local paper in my town offered me money to shop locally. He gave me some cash and I went to 10 downtown boutiques and bought stuff for myself, then wrote about the stores and all of their great deals. The shops loved the publicity. I loved my new clothes. It made me think I should have more experiences, so I continue to offer experience story ideas and have included a "Wine Tasting" story and "Get Pampered" column. You get the experience, the business owners get great publicity and your editor fills up a page with lots of great coverage of the community in a first-hand experience story!

Conference Speaker
You know the saying, 'anyone with a suitcase and 50 miles outside the city is an expert.' It's true. I don't necessarily consider myself an expert, but I do work hard, read a lot and try to stay current on all the latest social media trends. I wrote a couple of books about it and have been fortunate enough to travel all over the world and speak on the topic. The pay varies but the opportunities are amazing. Sometimes I get my hotel paid for and get to attend an incredible conference for free, in exchange for my one-hour presentation. Sometimes the organization pays for flight, hotel, food and writes me a check for speaking. Yes, people will pay you to talk. Sometimes I just get to network and make some really great friends and know that more opportunities will come from these meetings. How do you get these gigs? You can write a white paper, ebook or publish a book. Sometimes people will find you or refer you. You can actively google and search for conferences in your industry and look for the "Call for Speakers" tab. Simply submit a proposal. Make it relevant and exciting.

Start a Blog
Write what you know. Do you love gardening or cooking. Are you an entrepreneur and capable of helping other people get off the ground. Oh and guess what. You could charge blog for a business and charge a weekly fee to write and manage the blog, then you can start linking with online advertisers and help your new business owner make a little extra money. This is a great way to show them why they should keep you. While blogs are becoming passé in the world of new social, blogs with great 'search tags' are an amazing way to get your work recognized by the media and you could prove to be the expert journalists call on for quotes.

Write a Weekly Column for a Newspaper
If you notice a lot of people subscribed to your blog or you get a lot of likes on your witty facebook posts, it seems like you might be somewhat of an expert on something. Chances are, your local paper wants you to have your own column. Newspapers are dwindling in staff and barely have enough time to cover the events throughout your area, so a well-written regular column on a trendy, well-researched topic, would be a welcome gift to the publisher. You may or may not get paid, but at a minimum, you'll build your byline portfolio, get some new followers and become more visible in your industry. You do know that leads to consulting and speaking gigs right?

Design Websites
You don't have to know html code to put up a website. Sites like GoDaddy.com and Register.com offer template services for under $10 a month. Sell it to your client with an initial design fee, then add a monthly rate for weekly web content updates. If you have iWeb or another web design software and some graphic design skills, you can have more flexibility and design freedom, but you will have a bit of a learning curve with links, video uploads and layout. Average cost to design a website ranges from $2,000 to $10,000. Typically these web design rates includes experience with html code and SEO—search engine optimization. So if you are just starting out, focus on selling your services to new and small businesses that just want to have an online shingle. You could charge $200 to $500 for your template site, then a monthly or hourly fee for updates. $25 is a good hourly rate.

Publish a Book
You are an expert at something. What have you done for the past 10 or 20 years that you can teach others how to do? People pay to learn. They buy books and take classes all the time so they can be better at what they do, change careers, explore new trends and hone their hobbies. As a writer and publisher, I have taught a class called "How to Write and Publish an eBook in a day" (yes it's on Amazon). But here's the free scoop. Write down 10 things you know about a topic. Write down another 10. Go back and write a paragraph for each topic. Before you know it, you will have a book. Publish your eBook on Amazon's kindle or upload print version to Amazon's self-publish service CreateSpace. If you don't love technology, choose from any one of the self-publish services that will do it all for you—for a fee. But it is a way to make some royalties, on a monthly basis, for your expertise. (P.S. I publish books (more than 100 titles in the past decade) and will be happy to help you if the technology piece is too much jenny@thePubPlace.com).

Freelance Social Media
Every business owner knows they need to be on facebook, start tweeting and get LinkedIn, but not everybody knows how to do it. Sure, they might know how to set up a facebook page or sign up for an account but they are so busy running the day-to-day operations that they don't have the time or expertise to manage the social platforms that give them the online presence they need to be successful. Put together a launch package to set up the main social platforms, kick off an interactive and engaging campaign, then offer to manage the sites with regular posts. $500 - $1,000 for the initial set-up, then a monthly fee based on their needs. $200 - $500 monthly is an acceptable range for weekly managing posts, responding, interacting and hosting contests. Teenagers and young adults keep up with social trends, so they are good resources for helping you learn how to navigate these tools—if you need to catch up.

Contract Fundraiser
There are thousands of nonprofits looking for new ways to raise money for their cause. Some of them have a full-time fundraiser who is responsible for planning events, writing grants, getting sponsors, working on donor recruitment—and any number of tasks requiring their one-on-one interaction. If you could assume the role of planning and executing the annual gala, chili fest or offer up other new and unique ideas, a development director somewhere would love to give you ten percent of the dollars raised. You should start with your local nonprofits, but know there are many organizations worldwide that are just waiting for you to call them.

Fashion Consultant

If GrrrAnimals made a line of clothes for adults, there are people who should buy them. It's not a criticism, just an observation. I understand that some people are too busy to keep up with trends and others just don't have the knack for putting together the perfect ensemble every day, but everyone really does want to look good. If you have a sense of fashion and love to keep up with trends, you can help turn someone else's closet into a runway wardrobe. Start by asking for their goals. Do they want a new look? Do they want to move out of the black chapter? Have they seen this year's trends, tried them and just couldn't make it work? Help them re-invent with their current wardrobe, suggest a few pieces they could purchase to crank up their style. Charge a fashion makeover fee of $300 and offer four hours of your time for your fashion creative. No certificate or degree required. If updating your customer requires a shopping trip, add the 10 percent fee.

Online Educator

There are numerous online colleges offering undergraduate and graduate degrees. If you have a masters in something, then you are a master at something. University of Phoenix, Walden University, Strayer, and Kaplan are just a few of the colleges that are looking for great teachers who are comfortable teaching in an online environment. So, you only have a Bachelors degree? Well guess what? If you have a lot of experience in a particular field, there are a few colleges that will take a look at your credentials and evaluate if you are the right fit and will combine your BA with your life experience and let you wear a professor hat. Or, you can do something wild and crazy and start offering an online course. It's easy enough to set up a website and tap into the Blackboard site that colleges use and offer your expertise. There's a little work involved here, but you want to be professional and be at the top of your field, so people will refer future students. You will need a syllabus and a plan of execution. If you have an expertise in something not offered by traditional colleges, that's even better. Play around with the fees but know that in this tight job market, people are looking for certificates and skills to help sell themselves for jobs. Just because you aren't an accredited higher education facility, doesn't mean you aren't excellent at what you do. Go teach it and make some money. There are lots of certificates out there for a variety of career topics. While many don't have a higher education accreditation, some people are just looking for extensive education in particular topics.

Tech Consultant
There is a whole generation of boomers out there who want to be technically connected and have no idea where to start, but they are happy to pay you to move them into the twenty first century with their technology. You know enough to help them buy a new computer, hook up a printer, get a new phone and set up a facebook account so they can see their grandkids. They will gladly pay you a few hundred dollars to connect them. Then they will likely get on facebook and tell all of their friends about you because they still don't realize everyone sees the wall (might be the first thing you want to teach them). Word of mouth is always the best advertising.

Make and Sell Jewelry
Beads, bobbles, links and latches – you can google a bazillion how-to videos and make jewelry. There are really cool crimping tools in a little $10 kit Get some Modge Podge, ES 6000 and a hot glue gun and you are set to adhere, link, embellish and design your own line of jewelry. Come up with a cool name. Then get your new line up on ETSY and sell to the world. Who knows, you might create some new unique line that jewelry stores across America want to sell. With 'grow big' in mind, set retail prices and create a wholesale sheet for vendors. There are gift shows in cities nationwide that host 'market' dates. Jacob Javits in NYC has one of the biggest year-round gift shows in the US where jewelry makers schlep their items to store buyers nationwide. Most big cities have a 'market' with permanent locations and special events for store owners to come and buy in bulk. Get your paperwork ready with wholesale rates and purchasing minimums, then start taking orders.

Professional Food Taster or Taste-Tester
Culinary manufacturing organizations need taste testers. If you are 18 and have taste buds, you are in. Although some companies would prefer you have a culinary background, this can come in the form of cooking classes and extensive training so you can bring your fully knowledgeable palate to the table. It's not about liking or disliking what you try. You have to be able to discuss texture, flavor and palatability to name a few. The industry recommends you specialize in a certain area of foods and live a clean life – no smoking or drinking or messing with those valuable taste buds. Pay varies, but if you get one of these gigs, you are going to eat well and be the first to try a lot of foods.

Promotional Person
If you are of the attractive type, you should be out there where people can see you. Marketing agencies and promotional companies are always looking for pretty people to go out and gather information and introduce new products. From wine makers to pastry bakers, there are gigs for attractive people to draw people to a booth, display or tasting. This gig requires a little networking and googling, but the jobs are out there. Have a photo and resume ready and search promo gigs.

Grant Writer
No special training to write a grant. It's you telling a story about a nonprofit organization and providing proof of the 501.c3 nonprofit status. Grants (available online through a variety of websites like Grantstation and Chronicle of Philanthropy) provide you with the starting point—they tell you what they will give you money for. Then you write it up, just like they said, but adding the organization's information, creative idea, how you will execute it and how much money you want. It really is that easy. They give you a checklist of all the things you need to send and the deadline to send them. Nonprofits need money. Grants are a great way to get money, but nobody has time to write them. Meet with several nonprofits in your community and offer to find and write grants on a 10 percent commission basis—that you will include in the grant budget under personnel expense. Go write fancy grants, help nonprofits and make some extra cash.

Review Writer
Do you like giving your opinion? (pause). Okay, then great. If you have opinions on a lot of things, then chances are you are probably an avid reader. Why not get paid to read stuff then give your opinion in the form of a review. Google book gigs and find opportunities to provide reviews. You do have to buy the books and pitch to review sites, but then get paid to read books you would have bought.

Teach Abroad
Maybe you are a bit late on your rent or have a crazy ex stalking you. What better time to get out of the country and do something awesome to help others at the same time. Teaching English abroad is a great way to visit another country and get paid. Don't need a degree, but usually need to have to the TESL certificate. Japan is at the top of the needs list, but look around and go wherever you want to go.

Put Yourself on Tour
If you are a painter or photographer, the opportunities for you to put your collection on tour are incredible. Cities across America have spent the past decade turning their downtown areas into artisan hubs. Even the smallest of cities offers a row of art shops just clamoring for your collection. Put together an online portfolio of your artwork, your display fee (yes the gallery will pay you) or your percent offering for any artwork available for sell. Then share your tour on social sites and I bet you will get another one, and another one and another one.

Become a Ghostwriter
If you enjoy writing and telling stories, you are in business. There are a lot of people out there with a lot of great stories and they are waiting on someone to tell it for them. They will pay you money to listen to them, then tell their story. Then you could publish it for them as well. Getting an interview or someone's story can lead to you writing a book, getting published and even the basis for the next script of a movie.

Bike Tour Guide
There are companies looking for someone to join their bike tours and by bike I mean bicycle and by join, I mean bring your smart phone and do the social media for the company. Not only will you get to go on some nice bike rides in some nice countries, but you will get to help out with the social media, will get some airfare paid for and rack up some miles.

Nonprofit Leader
With more than 1.5 million organizations registered as nonprofits and out there raising dollars for their cause, somebody is always hiring. Just because they are nonprofit doesn't mean they are not-for-profit meaning there are always a group of passionate people running these organizations and everyone involved is out there raising money. If you have passion for a cause, go help! You could start out as a volunteer and work your way up to leader. I could introduce you to dozens of leaders who landed the top position by starting out as volunteers. Key word: passion. So consider helping an organization you love and recognizing it might turn into a full-time gig. If you are reading this book, chances are, you like to juggle and try out a few opportunities all at once. Many nonprofits offer a smaller salary and the flexibility to run the organization on a part-time basis, while doing some other things you love.

Social Analytics Consultant
Lots of marketing professionals and digital content producers are out there producing and making things happen and they don't have time to do the ROI or the analytics. Provide this service for a small monthly fee of $100. You just need login information for their website, facebook and social accounts. Then write up a little report—you can cut and paste the data easily presented by Google Analytics and facebook—and make the marketing professionals shine. Get 10 companies at this rate and for the few hours it takes to login and save the info, you can make a few extra bucks. I'm almost embarrassed at how easy this is and how much money you can make by 'social reporting.'

Virtual Assistant
Be a secretary to a BUNCH of bosses. If you are the organizational type and want to offer typing, data entry or be a virtual concierge, you can do all that from your cushy couch. There is a website set up that offers new jobs daily www.virtualassistantjobs.com and you can pick and choose the jobs you want, the people you want to work for and the hours and projects that interest you.

Home Call Center
If you have a computer, a phone and some thick skin, you could run a virtual call center. Jobs are posted en masse on Career Builder and Indeed.com on a regular basis. With more and more companies outsourcing call centers, they finally realize people can do this from home. While dealing with customer issues may not sound like a dream job, it is one you can do from home, with flexible and varied schedules and a way to make a little extra money. Your dog will be happy to have you there all day.

Electronic Clipping Service
Companies are busy sending out press releases and trying to get daily media coverage. They used to have a person or an intern or someone who had time to peruse every newspaper and publication to find, clip and store any news piece mentioning the company. Technology has made clipping even easier and can be done from anywhere. Using Google Alert, you can receive news articles in your inbox to click and print or save to a CD or Dropbox. Pitch yourself to mid-sized and large companies on a contract basis. Get a few companies to say YES and you will have a great new source of income for something you do on your own schedule.

Digital Organizer
Companies keep buying file cabinets in an effort to house the paperwork they can't physically bear to part with. The IRS doesn't even want you keep paperwork for more than 3 years, so why are you? If you love organizing, this is your opportunity to digitally organize a company. Easy scanning technology will let you scan and save page by page as jpgs and PDFs, then store on a CD or external hard drive –or both. If a company still has paper invoices and contracts from the 1980s, they will need to know it is exists in multiple locations and assorted formats. Then create a nice index – you can do that in Microsoft Word and present it in a neatly packaged portfolio. Charge by the hour or per project!

Photography Organizer

Years ago, we went took our film to the store to get it developed and could hardly wait to see the prints, which we then organized in albums and boxes, neatly dated and categorized. Now we snap a photo with our smart phone and upload to our facebook and twitter feed and have no physically printed memories of our personal life, let alone our businesses. It's nice to know they are in the CLOUD, but 20 years from now, a new CEO is going to roll in and ask to see pictures from your past 10 galas. Good luck finding those! There is a need and I know this because I just hired someone to do it. Pay someone to visit your facebook, twitter and flickr sites, vine, instagram, whatever you use and send them to print and organize them in real boxes that sit on a real shelf.

Personal Shopper
I know it sounds crazy, but some people do NOT like to shop. They would be happy to pay you a fee to go out and buy the perfect gifts for their friends, family members and office associates. Pop up a website and share it on your social sites. Average fees are 10% per order, with minimum of $25 per shopping trip.

Scarf Maker

I know it might not sound like a lucrative opportunity but people pay a lot of money for handmade gifts. If you can knit, then get those needles going. Or, maybe you are like me and you are better at applying things. You can go to Hobby Lobby and get the scrap booker and hair design products and hot glue and stitch them to inexpensive scarves you purchased at the dollar store. Sell them on ETSY and to your local boutiques. Create a really cool name for your items and promote them as vintage, one-of-a-kind, boutique items and add a few extra dollars to the retail price. People pay for handmade!

Gift Shop GIFTY Creator

Every town has two or three gift shops featuring a collection of, well, a lot of unique stuff. If you are of the crafty type, you could make a bazillion different things. Soaps, jams, stationery, clothes, hats, hand-painted items –the gift shop is your creative oyster. Create a wholesale sheet—a professional list of the items you want your local gift shops to sell. Give them a retail price (so they will know what to sell it for), then half that for the wholesale rate (this is the amount they pay you at delivery or when your items sell). Value your time when pricing the items. Remind yourself that people love handmade. Take time for labels and packaging to make your items as unique and special as possible.

Recruiter/Hiring Firm
If you go on Monster, Career Builder or any other job board, you often see multiple jobs posted by the same company. These are agencies or hiring firms. Why not start your own? If there is an industry you know a lot about, you can certainly start there. Get a website with 4 tabs. One with a list of jobs (you can create from other job boards), another with a place for an employee to submit their resume. You match them up.

Wine Glass Painter

Although I consider myself artistic, I can't seem to master painting on a flat surface and making it not look like I'm in kindergarten. I cannot paint with acrylic, oils or watercolors on a canvas. However, I have discovered that I can paint on wine glasses. It started out as a fun way to crank up a wine tasting fundraiser but has evolved into an obsession. You can buy inexpensive cases of wine glasses, then Embellish paint for glasses—it comes in many colors. Buy a few paint pens specific for glass. Then paint, bake and sell. You spend $1 on a wine glass, add your art and charge $20 like Lolita does. People love customized gifts.

Become a Sommelier

Drink and learn about wine. A lot. I mean, drink a lot AND learn a lot. Consider yourself a matchmaker of sorts. Your job is to get to know people and learn about what they like then match them with the perfect wine. You could offer your services on an individual basis or as a consult to restaurants that serve wine. While you may already have some industry experience—ordering for a restaurant or in a catering role—you can always go online and get the Master Sommelier certificate. The term expert may mean different things to different clients, so your vast knowledge of grape varietals, vineyards and wines may be enough to get you a gig. According to the Court of Master Sommeliers, there is a membership with 214 people worldwide. It's a really small club and an opportunity for you to get some gigs. Yes there is an exam (touted one of the hardest) and it probably includes correct spelling of 'sommelier.'

Crime Scene Cleaner

I once saw a movie with Morgan Freeman in it and he actually did this for a living. I did a little research and discovered that in fact these jobs pay big bucks. If you aren't squeamish, feel comfortable sporting a Hazmat suit and don't mind a little detail work, this is a perfect job for you. There's no real degree required, though some companies offer certifications, but if your profession has been in the safety industry or you've worked in the trauma unit of a hospital, chances are you have the perfect skill sets to clean up the aftermath of a crime.

Brewmaster

You could become a certified Brewmaster or you could get some microbrewery products and kits and do it yourself at your house. It's now easier than ever to purchase bottles and design your own labels. Designing your own brew certainly makes you the favorite neighbor at backyard barbecues. However, if formal education and discovering all the potentials of your fermentation frenzy is on your list, there is an American Brewers Guild with a 27-week program—21 online and a 5-week apprenticeship at nationwide breweries. There is also a Siebel Institute of Technology with a 12-week program to make you a Beer master. So whether you home brew or intern at a big brewery and get the certificate, you can make a great beer. Brew it. Drink it. It's like having one hobby that supports your other hobby.

Professional Sleeper
Yes this is a dream job and you have all the experience you need. Hotel chains periodically hire sleepers. They want you to spend about 30 days at their hotel and go from room to room and just sleep. Well you get to eat too and watch television and movies, but you are there to provide your feedback on your experience. In addition to hotels, lots of research on sleep patterns opens doors for you to snooze for bucks. Google sleep research for opportunities.

Resort Jobs
While you are checking out hotel jobs, there certainly are some unique opportunities for getting paid and working at a fancy resort. The Peabody, in several cities, has a Duckmaster, who manages the ducks that do a morning and evening parade throughout the hotel. I've personally seen this impressive sight and now impressed to know there is a duck supervisory opportunity out there waiting for me. Other unique resort jobs include an onsite sunglass doctor who will shine and repair your glasses, a soap concierge who ensures guests get the best slippery sensory slice of handmade soaps and a tanning concierge who will monitor and advise for your best fake spray or protected natural tan. Visit websites of large hotels worldwide to find these unique opportunities.

Private Investigator
Sleuthing has never been easier than in today's world of technology. While having a degree in criminal justice or appropriate courses in human behavior and criminology can certainly enhance opportunities to work for some big companies, one out of every four PIs is self-employed. Opportunities can range from field surveillance to locate assets, workers comp investigations, property theft and identity fraud. Some of the skill sets to make you successful in this field include a quiet stealthy manner, ability to lie, clean background (so you can carry a gun) and strong organizational skills. You can make around $50,000 annually on a full-time basis, but if you want to do a little sligh PI on the side and help catch your best friend's cheating husband

Body Parts Model

Aristotle said the 'whole is more than the sum of its parts,' but that's because he didn't realize some of its parts were worth a lot of money in solo gigs. We know the runway wants 5'8" and taller, but there are a lot of opportunities to model individual parts of your body. Do you have great hands or feet? How about your eyes? Anyone ever brag on your gorgeous knees? There are a variety of skin, body and make-up manufacturers looking for great body parts to help highlight and market their products. Websites representing body part models tout as many as 14 divisions, opportunities to email full body and part-specific photos as well as stop by for open auditions.

Phone Actress
It's acting with your voice. There is a website recruiting fantastic voice talent for telecommunications company at www.phoneactress.com. This gig offers weekly checks and flexible hours and pays you for your amazing voice. Be careful when you google this, because you could end up as an Adult Phone Entertainer. Yes, this is a separate opportunity that pays cash because there are people who are lonely and for one reason or another, want to have intimate conversations with a stranger. In the movie "Valentine's Day," Anne Hathaway held this position as her part-time gig while looking for a real job.

Write for Dumb People

Dumb people are everywhere and according to a publisher with nearly 2,000 different titles on any topic imaginable geared to help people not be dumb, it offers you an opportunity to write. You are likely an expert at something and could lead the effort or contribute to a book. Google "Write for dummies" to submit your credentials, writing samples and experience and they will keep it on file to match you up with their next great book.

Fancy Dress Rental
Moms spend hundreds of dollars getting their teenage girls ready for proms, homecomings and other fancy dances with a dress that gets worn one time. The tech-savvy moms put them on eBay or takes them to a consignment shop, but for the most part, the dresses hang out in a spare closet for years and years. Have a big dress recruitment event and collect dresses, take pics and put up a website. You will save moms lots of money, girls will still get to wear a one-of-a-kind dress at an affordable rate and you will have cleaned up your community of its fancy dress deluge. Don't forget your charitable part – and share with those in need.

Toy Tester
Not the easiest job to get, but if you get connected and do a thorough job, you will get paid to play! These jobs aren't usually posted on career boards, so be prepared to do a little cyber sleuthing on toy store websites. Companies want feedback for new toys they plan to sell, so they want to know how it works, if it is age appropriate and mentally challenging. They want comprehensive feedback before they purchase in bulk and spend lots of money marketing a new item. If you have some little ones in your house, it is a great way to build your toy box.

Traveling Artist
If you sing, dance, paint or play an instrument, freelance opportunities are everywhere. Performing arts centers and schools are always looking for ways to expand the art programs they offer and will pay to do it. Schools no longer have full-time art or music teachers and are scrapping to find ways to enhance the arts. Typically, they have grants to fund it. So put together a portfolio of arts academy classes you can teach and email your offerings to any organization or school within your traveling circle. Every state has an arts council and will help promote your services for free and often provide funding to the recipients in the form of grants. This is a great way to make a little extra cash, do some networking and expand your teaching portfolio.

Virtual Fitness Instructor
Do you know how many people never start exercising because they don't want to go to a gym? If you are a little overweight or a little out of shape, the last thing you want to do is go struggle through a workout in front of everyone. People like privacy and there is no day like today for delivering services right through your computer. If you have a background in Pilates or Yoga, weight lifting or good ole jazzercise, you can open your own online studio. A Virtual gym or studio offering private lessons is easy with SKYPE or USTREAM. While Skype lets you provide one-on-one training in an intimate PC environment, you'll need to set up a method to receive payments. (Square is a quick and easy free APP that lets you accept credit cards). To offer classes to large groups of people, Ustream provides a pay-perview service, you'll split the fee 50/50 but it's an easy way to help the masses get healthy.

Market Researcher
If you have a bit of an investigative, puzzle-solving mind, market researcher is the job for you. In this huge field that spans all industries, there are facts and numbers to be gathered. If spreadsheets get your juices bubbling and collecting data puts you on a natural high, this is your gig. You could be the data gatherer, analyzer, evaluator, surveyor or part of a variety of focus groups. Just google the topic and the opportunities are endless and no degree required.

Zamboni Driver
Ice sport enthusiasm and a little patience are the only requirements to drive a Zamboni. By bravery, I mean, the machine travels an average of three miles per hockey game with a top speed of 9.7 mph and can go from zero to ¼ mile in 93.5 seconds. With more than 10,000 Zamboni machines sold and delivered around the world, somebody probably needs a driver. Find your nearest ice rink and just ask. I have no idea what the pay is but how cool would it be to resurface ice in front of thousands of hockey fans- and I bet there would be some free tickets involved.

Trade Show Organizer

Companies go to trade shows on a regular basis to get the word out about their company, products or services. If you have a nice suit, an inviting smile, can learn quickly and enjoy traveling and meeting new people, this job is for you. Entrepreneurs and new companies are seeking every opportunity they can to get their new biz out in front of everyone that matters and sometimes they need an extra person. I once went to a bicycle trade show in Vegas and ran a booth for an entrepreneur who had invented the no-nose bicycle seat. I spent several weeks reading and learning everything I could about the product and the industry, then flew to the west coast, popped up the display and went to work. As the representative for this entrepreneur, it was important for me to shake a lot of hands, show off the seat, generate excitement for our targeted audience and more importantly get business cards and contacts for follow up. Compensation varies, but it's a great way to visit big cities and meet new people. If you get some regular gigs, plan to spend some time in Vegas and Atlanta—a couple of hubs for conferences.

Gaming Surveillance Observer
If you live near a casino and are a bit of a gambler, then there's an opportunity for you to make some money—without gambling away your own dollars. Observers work for specific casinos to monitor and record gambling activities and ensure that the company's assets are safe. You must be 21 and complete a gaming card registration. You'll be paying such close attention to detail, that you might end up learning a thing or two in the gambling world and find yourself as the next card shark expert. You'll get paid to pay attention.

Video Maker for You Tube
If you have a smart phone with a camera, you have all the equipment you need to get started in this business. If you have a hobby or skill that you can share with others, you are off to a career on You Tube. (Oh and set up a Pay Pal account if you don't already have one so you can get paid.) Then prop up your camera and start teaching people how to do things. Do you cook? Do you have a garden? Do you have a technical skill or expertise in a software? Make a three to five minute video on a particular topic in your field, then upload it to You Tube. Use all the free publicity tools on the site and start getting people to follow you. In the settings, click 'monetize' and advertisers with a connection to your topic, will link to your video. Every time someone views your video, You Tube will put a little money in your PayPal account. You can even sign up to become a You Tube Partner where you will get access to more creative tools and have a chance to win prizes. The more videos you make, the more money that will trickle in your account.

Fluffer

Okay, I saved this for the end. It was the reason I started writing this book years ago in its working title "Careers Your Mother Never Told You About." I learned about Fluffers on, none other than, the Discovery Channel in some documentary that went behind the scenes for a pornographic movie. A fluffer is the person who ensures the actor is perky—at all times. The best way to get one of these jobs is to move to an area with film studios producing such films, so head west my friend.

www.ingramcontent.com/pod-product-compliance
Lightning Source LLC
Chambersburg PA
CBHW051728170526
45167CB00002B/845